A Collection of Ashes

Kim Germsheid

xoxo

To be understood
is one of life's greatest feelings
seen
held
heard

I hope you feel that in these words

Dedication

This collection is for all of you who have ever felt "too much" and "not enough" all at the same time. For those who dance within the edges of the flames, not afraid to get burned. To those who are discovering themselves and who have felt lost along the way. May you find your light within written in the words of this book.

Table of Contents

Chapter One
Burning Embers

BURSTING IN FLAMES

I am on the divine path of my calling
I am invested and aligned
I am calling my sisters home
my heart is bursting and on fire

IN FLOW

I am more myself than I have ever been before
more in tune
more in the groove of my path
more focused on what it is that I am calling in

I am motivated by much of the past
all of those who never believed in me
the ones who teased me for being different
those who pushed me away into isolation

I feel brave for the ones who weren't able to be
the ones that were ruled by cycles and patterns
those that felt the hand of oppression
they who felt there was no way out

I stay close to who I am for both sides
the ones who helped form me into the Phoenix that I have become
crawling out of the ashes
sprawling across the sky

I do this for me
to prove that I've always had it

always been worthy
and even more badass
than I could ever imagine

Led By The Heart

When your heart is led
to those who speak the language of your soul
it makes that fire burn just a little hotter

BEAUTY OF THE FLAMES

The thing about flames, is no one asks questions
no one stands in its way
asking for an explanation
they watch with terror in their eyes
but there isn't an expectation to change
as fire takes what it wants

so I have been hiding the flames that make up my being
afraid to appear selfish
too powerful, seen
bringer of pain

after flames, comes the rebirth
a fresh start
the fruitful soil that is left behind
allowing the precious flowers
to grow
in place of the jungle of vines that were

what people forget about is the beauty that comes

fire presents in so many forms
there is no peace without destruction
the contrast of the world
is needed to be able to see through the lens
to find the magic
of all the beauty that surrounds us

FLAMES OR WATER

As someone who has always been too much
I live within the extremes
all or nothing
too high or too low
flames or water

I wouldn't change a thing

LEFT BEHIND

I walk away from the flames that reach out of every crevice
as the water sprays over it seeps into every crack
washing away all evidence of belonging
another charred ember hits the air

I listen to the voices of those fighting
working to save the things I worked and saved for
all the memories are beginning to evaporate
washing down the hall to where they don't belong

I say goodbye to what once was, what will never again be
I keep my eyes fixated on moving forward
I wipe the black from my forehead
and a trail is left down my cheek- wet and cold

just like all my treasures left behind in the darkness
I bravely walk out into the cold street
into the unknown with absolute certainty
that nothing will ever be the same again

LIGHTHOUSE

I have wandered
many dark and lonely halls
through the desolate wheat fields

searching
looking for a way out
a way in
a light in the darkness
as mine had been extinguished
the breath of darkness too fierce

on that dark and dusty road
I saw it- a flicker
as I journeyed toward it my flames came to life
feeding off the frenzy
only this time
I allowed the fire to grow
as the tendrils curled and climbed
I surrendered to the fire
allowed it to consume all that I was
I let it in, welcomed it
for a taste of sweet whisky
listening to it's voice as it consumed my flesh

and then quiet, I extinguished the flames that enraged my
body, my mind

with the ability to hold the flicker in my hand
using it to ignite my passions and purpose
I buried the ashes of the past
creating the abundant soil from which I rose
a hauntingly beautiful scarlet Phoenix

holding the wisdom within each feather
I found my magic
a lighthouse,
helping others to discover where they left their lantern

exploring the depth of the caves, offering a light
lending the glow of my flame to expose the shadows
and inviting them along for the journey

no longer afraid
showing them how to protect their flame
when the breath gets too heavy
being there to relight the torch
knowing that the darkness is easier to navigate
when there is a light shining for you
illuminating the Earth to see their footsteps

LONGING

Oh the longing
to feel your fingers tracing old familiar paths atop my warm
skin
the way you make me melt into an endless puddle onto your
floor
you've always had your ways

your eyes are imprinted on the backs of my eyelids
your words swirl within my mind
I have a sickness
an incurable disease
and you hold the only antidote
in the palm of your hands

SPARKS

When I was young
I played with matches
not knowing
that all these years later
it was the fire that gave me the spark
to be who I truly am
myself

LOVING BEAUTY

Her heart is one with the world
feeling too deeply
loving too hard
she loves fiercely with passion in her eyes
soft and tender
her heart beats for all of those lost, already gone

her mouth full of eloquently formed words
words bursting with compassion and inspiration
guiding souls to come home to themselves

her hair red like flames
reminding her of her power and presence
channelling her inner mermaid
swimming within

her feet have moved her through many dances in life
some fun and entertaining
some slow and tragic
always helping her take one step forward at a time

her arms have held many anguished hearts

offering support and gentle care to those who cross her path
unconditional and fierce

I haven't always held such grace for her, finding her many flaws
too thick, stretched, curvy to fit the mold I tried to enclose her
even still
she has risen
claiming her space in the world
like the queen that she is

not always feeling worthy, enough, or complete
her soul has expanded to hold the pieces together when they
wanted to fall
the gold was slowly painted on each of the lines

her home, her safe space, her world
all created within these walls of her delicate worldly curves
she feels cradled and cared for when she goes within

warrior woman, goddess of fire
she is who came before
birthing the wisdom within
breaking down old barriers, cycles and generational trauma
loving beauty never forget your power

your truth
your essence

BLEEDING

You need to bleed to burn

THIRSTY TO BURN

She sneaks out like a teenager in the night
hunting her next prey
she has her wicked tongue lashing
slapping anyone in her way
venomous and fierce

I run to try to capture her
my feet char as they beat against the earth
for she has lit up a path of flames
wanting to burn it all to the ground
and if I'm not careful
she may succeed once again

a few chapters ago in this book
she was a welcomed friend

she provided protection from evil
creating the most secure barrier
boiling and searing the prying fingers
leaving blisters upon their wagging tongues

I know if I'm not careful
she can sneak back out of this house
and leave it behind in a pile of ash
finding a new home to repeat her anarchy

thirsty to burn, smoke and ruin

hungry for devastation
always burning
waiting
watching

Boldly Burning

I choose to burn hotter
to weed out
those too scared of the uncomfortable
afraid of the heat

TRUTH

What is truth anyway?
truth is not something we get a healthy dose of
in the current society we live
it's almost trendy to "fake it til you make it"
which I tried for a long time

truth is
I never knew what "making it" even meant
what was the marker in the sand
to know when I made it?

I have stumbled and fallen to my knees
more times than can be counted
I've had my heart handed back
in more pieces than when I gave it
tried, lied and cried more times that I know
pretended I was someone I wasn't

begged
for a taste of the exquisite gruel they were serving
asked for a second helping
time and time again

I put FOR SALE signs in the windows of my mind

I allowed the highest bidders to move in
never evicting the delinquent tenets that had settled
at the front of my shelves
doubt/self-loathing/self-pity
spices that I seasoned every dish with
I kept the fire that raged on within my flesh
a well kept secret
if the flames of fury had ever escaped
it would swallow up the entirety of my world

if one thing is for certain
it's that I fought my way back to my feet
more times than I was pushed to the ground

I grew strong in the fertile ash I created
resilient to the core, a fighter
but this time for me

I took the FOR SALE signs down
wanting to be the sole owner
truth is, I'm a work in progress
and that, I know, is the goal
the marker in the sand
to become stronger, better, and wiser
as the days go by

BEAUTIFUL MESS

I'm not always tied up in a neat package
put together for viewing
I'm an emotional being
I let all the pieces fall to the floor

shattered-I have cried the tears of agony
that cut just a little deeper each time
I have felt the fury of the fiery rage
flames hot enough to scorch small villages

needy, lonely and afraid to be in solitude
stifled and cagey
don't come too close
not knowing what I want or what I don't want
angry with the world

I can be jealous and filled with envy
competitive and controlling
I have been immature and petty
especially when wronged

the beauty of this whole mess
is that it's part of who we are
complete with the entirety of feelings
that come to us, time after time

FIRE TO ASH

Memories destroyed by fire
washed away by water
burned to ash
evaporated into air
as if they never existed

but you can't burn me down
I'll do that myself

BATHED IN FLAMES

To those lips that feel like home
the gaze that feels like sunshine
my heart burns for yours
bathed in flames

SETTING THE FIRE

I am ready to answer the call of my heart
bringing my truth to the world
to set more souls on fire

ASHES

Red glowing embers
the eyes of my nightmares
smother me in smoke
flames wrap tightly around my neck
sirens deafen my ears
ashes fall lightly on my tongue

WHAT ONCE WAS

I saw you today
you didn't look like yourself
empty and sad
stripped of all that filled you up
made you complete
standing there all alone

abandoned

your exterior being torn away
exposing the bare bones on the inside
taken down
dismantled
you need some time to recover

rest

this has been the most ravaging year
out of all your years
engulfed in a burst of flames

and now all that's left
is the darkness of the night
that you carry on your fractured shoulders

NIGHT GIVES WAY TO FLAMES

And in the blink of an eye
the night gives way to the flames
the air is consumed with thick black smoke

my life forever changed

SHADOW IN THE FIRE

I used to fear the fire I created around me
and now
I dance in the flames

reclaiming my power
as a fiery being
knowing that my journey
through the flames
is what makes me – me
it's what brings my vulnerability out to play

no longer fearing the flames
allows me to bring my fire medicine to the world
light in darkness

to be able to share the flames
in the words that I create
gentle yet fierce
truth

the glow from the embers
bringing light to the edges
the shadows I walked in
being illuminated

sharing all of me, as me
the shadow in the fire

Burning Brighter

I'm here to tell you
burn brighter
keep reaching your flames higher
and never, ever give up

COLD ABANDONMENT

The cold wind blows through piles of leaves
red, orange and yellow
they remind me of fire
flames

the ones that rip through my mind
burning down the old

all that's left
is a pile of abandonment

BEAUTY OF THE BURN

Keep burning
never snuff yourself
find a way to turn destruction
into beauty

Passion

I'm either burning it all down

or engulfed in passion

you decide

FEATHERS OF FLAMES

I wasn't always the Phoenix
I had to light many fires
be swallowed by the flames
in order to find my feathers

HEART OF FLAMES

This heart of mine is wild
an animal roaming in the jungle
fighting like an ancient warrior woman
for all she believes to be true

her walls consumed in fire
passion dripping from her fingertips
she sheds her light brightly over the dark sea
for she does nothing without intensity

she has been eaten alive and left for dead
vultures picked the flesh off her bones
she's feasted on prey in the darkness of the night
overtaken by lust and desire

my heart has been my rock-steady
never giving way under the weight of the world
she loves fiercely and freely
wildflowers spread across her canvas

she has taken a few wrong turns along the way
but has always steered us back onto the road
we hold each other as we weave our way through
she beats her music, the soundtrack of my life

FIRE AND ICE

The taste of your words
takes over my mind
consumed by your fire and ice
wanting more
always

dreaming
thinking
yearning
always within the confines of my mind

hungry and craving
the heat of the your flames

FLAMES OF LUST

Woo me with magic
speak to me the language of the moon
caress me with your Phoenix feathers
and I will fan your flame

TOWARDS THE FIRE

The only way to clear your mind
you must follow the fireflies
out of the cave
towards the fire

let the fire ignite your heart
and allow it to ravage the hurt
feed it oxygen it needs
to create an inferno

breathe life into it
allow your insides to pour out into flames

watch as it consumes each element
self-doubt, maliciousness and poisonous venom
aching loneliness, abandonment and unkindness
trauma, unjust and evil of the world

admire the boldness of the tendrils
reaching higher into the sky
than you ever thought possible

then it's quiet
the world goes silent
as you are crowned your wings
-fly

Chapter Two
Growing Into Me

In My Skin

Beneath this skin
is all the magic
I'll ever need

FREE SPIRIT

I am a free spirit
one with the wind
flowing with each breath
higher and farther
free

I grow like wildflowers
with no real place to belong
scattered and spontaneous
free

I stay up too late
peering at the moon

I sleep too long
swept up in the dream side world

I laugh a little too loud
and allow passion to take over my words

I'm messy

allowing my creativity to take up space
I am a truth speaker
a black sheep
not afraid to break cycles
and set us all free

I am me
free

Nightmares

Long nights
lead to longs days
one day they will get easier
until then
I will be
with my nightmares

TRYING TO BE SEEN

Pink hair bows and dresses
were never my jam
from a tender age
I knew that my path was something different

I hated Barbies
and being treated as a fragile girl
I loved to get messy, covered in dirt
play with cars in the sandbox
and run wild in the streets
I was my happiest
with wild hair, wearing my overalls

I somehow saw the injustice and inequality
I saw the freedom the boys around me had
I knew I would always spend my life
trying to prove myself

I longed to be a boy
knowing it would always be the easier path

I spent so much of my time
trying to be seen and recognized
working hard to have a business
earning designations to even the unfair pay gap
trying not to talk too much
that's 'not what professional men do'

working hard
I never felt there was any other way
to be seen as an equal
to be viewed as an intellect

SISTER OF WORDS

I feel the nudge
whispers in the air
"keep going"
"keep looking"
"you will find it"

I happen upon a sister of words
a sister of life's art and beauty
an instantaneous knowing

we share our dreams
and leave inspiration
planted within the soil of our souls

my heart is bursting
on fire and smouldering
ready to set fire to my dreams
my calling
my passion

ALWAYS WITH ME

As the frost lifts on an early spring morning
he takes his last breath
my role model, my hero
King of adventure

I wasn't ready, I never would be
13- such a tough time for a young girl
I was crushed, heartbroken
desperate for answers

I remember how much my heart ached
ached for more days spent together on the farm
ached for the life teachings you had planned

how empty the world suddenly was without you

my story went dark, my eyes got blurry
depression consumed me
I wanted to be where you had gone
I prayed to be taken

I was done, wanted out
I cried and I cried
tired of being in pain
tired of the cruel world
things were never the same
our lives were empty
our hearts a little darker
my hope a little farther

years went by until I met you again
this time a little differently
only when I turned inward
could your presence be felt

it was that frosty spring morning
when I gained a Guardian Angel
a Spirit Guide
the one I talk to in the quiet of the night

you are always with me, always have been
you've stopped my tears
you've saved my life
and you've always loved me

BLAZING IN THE SHADOWS

Tenderness trickles from her eyes
the pain of the world is carried in her bones
where the only remedy is to hold more love for each other
our division continues blazing in the shadows

OLD DUSTY COMPASS

Old dusty compass has the directions
but doesn't expose the secret of which way I am to
travel
it spins its needle
'round & 'round
until I decide my path

GRIEF

I'm sad for the brokenness
the little girl that had no voice
never allowed to get too close to the edge
who crawled into small spaces
searching for her own place in the world
that was safe and far away
I cry for the woman
who learned that in order to be loved
you needed to be a certain way
conditional to the end
the woman who didn't learn how to feel
numbing with whatever gasoline there was
who still waits for the midnight sun
to let out any forbidden tears
the only true friends
the ones high in the sky
shining a caressing light
I grieve the lonely road
the single lane cloaked in darkness
headlights busted out
shards of glass still hanging out of the sockets
the rickety car that has always run on fumes
huffing for air
grasping for anything
to just keep going

DAYDREAMIN'

Among the marshmallow fluff
as they shapeshift to their heart's desire
maybe a mermaid, maybe a tree

free
transforming in the wind

I watch the sparkle of our dear stars
they blink in wonderment
burning bright
guiding us along our journey

daydreamin'

THE DEPTHS OF THE OCEAN

Sometimes I feel like I'm drowning in a teacup
if I just lift my head it would be easier
other times I feel like I'm deep
deep within the ocean

TRAVELLER

I'm a traveller
I travel the night skies within the dream realm to meet others whom my soul has a craving for. The universe has endless possibilities and no destination is too far. This space allows for both past and present souls to appear and go the journey together. There is no plausible explanation for what happens during this time.

I travel amongst the clouds on the wings of birds. I become weightless as I allow my soul to explore with them. I empty my mind and soar above all of my problems and life's responsibilities. Above mountain tops, over the big blue sea and across the desert. Reminded of the beauty life has to offer.

I travel to my past experiences. When I open my heart to my journey, there are cracks that allow me to travel back to soothe my inner child. She awaits my arrival as I come with the self love that I was not able to find before. The roads that I travel finding forgiveness are lined with lush green fields.

On the fence my inner child sits to await my return.

I travel within my mind, daydreaming of endless possibilities. My mind's eye has dreams and goals and destinations that it harbours. I journey within to add to my road map. I make notes to celebrate along the way.

I TRY

I try too hard
try not to take things to heart
try to keep my chin up
try to stay in my own lane
try to love myself
try to believe in me
try not to believe the "have-nots" in my mind

I try and I try
to not tear down
all of which I have built
burning it down to the ground
I try not to light the match

MEMORY

I look to the sky
searching for a sign
in between the twinkling diamonds
and the sweeping fluffs of cloud
I stretch my sight beyond
the earthly realm
for you have surpassed this level
you are seated amongst the greats
and down here in this visceral world
my heart aches

I miss you

NOT ENOUGH

"You're too much" sounds oddly the same as "I'm not good enough"
with every "you're weird" or "too loud"
I feel less and less ok with who I am

I was always a little more quirky than those around me
a little more rare
I heard all about how quiet my cousins were
and how pretty they were in photos

I was too thin, too loud and not "girly" enough
my clothes were never quite right and my hair was always too short
I never felt pretty enough, smart enough or cool enough
always looking for the magic puzzle piece, the one that would make me feel complete

as more time went by, I lost more pieces of the unfinished puzzle
breaking away
each not wealthy enough, not independent enough
and not thin enough
yanked away another piece

I am slowly gathering those pieces up
and finding where they lay

as I found the missing puzzle piece
the one that was always lost
it was never in the puzzle box

but deep within my soul

Inspiration

You are the inspiration for my words

the encouragement to keep going

and the courage to go for my dreams

TOO MUCH

Too much
too much talking, speaking words of love and inspiration
too much laughing, the sound of healing my deeply cut
wounds
too much excitement, a passion held for life and leading it to
better things
too much weight, a soft heart and body to hug and
encourage others
too much emotion, empathy like no one else you will meet
I am too much, but why does it need to be a bad thing?
I have more than I can ever use
so I openly give away as much as I can

SWALLOWED WHOLE

How foreign these feelings are
to have lost it all
and to feel more complete
swallowed whole by the fire
spit out with urgency
with a desire
to know that
the only thing impossible to lose
is myself
when everything disappears
it's me
the only thing that matters
exists

NEVER GIVING UP

As I sit here in the darkness
quiet surrounds me
the chaos of the world falls away
I am still

the clock ticks
reminding me to forge ahead
without condition
never giving up

I hear my breath
slow and steady
forceful yet gentle
never giving up

thoughts flood my mind
replaying the day
all the triumphs and challenges
never giving up

when I sit here in the dark
my dreams become bright
closer than they've ever felt
never giving up

MAGIC

To those of you who feel lost
after finishing the last page of that book
to those that look for seashells
while strolling at dusk on the beach
to those who love the feel of being transported
while sipping cappuccino in an indie cafe
to those who enjoy what's written between the lines
and who see animals in the clouds
to those who try again tomorrow
no matter what happened yesterday

my heart is with you who freely share
in the vulnerability of life
those who discover miracles
in life's most mundane places

there is magic to be seen
if only we allow our hearts to take it in

I AM

I am light
and I am shadow
I have it all together
and I unravel apart
I am strong
and I am emotional
I am free
and I am bound by shame
I am confident
and riddled with self-doubt
I am enough
and I fall short
I am brave
and I am fearful
I go after my dreams
and allow my nightmares to chase me
I am a work in progress
I am me

ARTIST

I always have words floating in my mind
piecing themselves together
to create a story of inspiration

pain, love, transformation
hopeful to better the world
one stanza at a time

my Maybelline lipstick in the shade *"Artist"*
poetry being a constant thread through life
always my way to express myself
the way the messages come to me
from the world beyond

GO THROUGH

It's the quiet days
when thoughts become loud

when we stop to take a breath
that it starts to feel hard to breathe

remember that we need time to feel
it's necessary for us to heal

no one will ever tell you
that the road will be easy

you must go through
through the cobwebs that were spun in the darkness
through mud and muck that coats your insides
through the tall cornfields
that swallow you whole
when you find yourself alone

you must fight through the waves
intensified by mother moon
when they strike you in the face
stinging the ego more than the skin

thoughts become louder
skies become darker
unless you listen to the thunder

there is no way out

breathe
go through
that's the only way to quiet the noise

WHAT IT FEELS LIKE

I can't tell you what it is
but I can tell you what it feels like

it feels like seeing the reflection of a sunrise
on the dewy blades of grass
it's like hearing your favorite band
when you turn on the radio

a warm cup of cocoa
after a cold winter's walk
like waking on a weekend
to the smell of coffee brewing

it feels like how your heart soars
when the eagle flies above you
it feels like the joy of a child's smile
graceful like the ocean's tide

when you gaze upon the night's sky
witnessing the aurora borealis
to watch a falling star
and bathe in the glow of the moon

how it feels to receive a letter

from a long time friend
the taste of maple syrup on your tongue
and sinking your feet in a tub of hot water

I can't tell you what it is
but I can tell you what it feels like

WILD WOMAN

I'm a wild woman
I color outside the lines
my flames cannot be contained
I'm a woman on fire

my wildness cannot be measured
my spirit spreads like dandelion seeds
blowing and scattering in the wind

I love to laugh obnoxiously
until tears stream down my face
cramps in my side
the volume deafening

I grow like the wildflowers
in any location I wish
whatever color I please
without rules

BEFRIENDING MY FEARS

Nightmares come to be
from all the avoided feelings
during the day
all the words
stuffed so deep within
that they must seep out
in the night
they are made from
all the words your voice longs to say
all the years worth of swallowing
the mistreatment, abuse, pain

if I make friends with these feelings
in the daytime
will they allow me peace
in the night?

STRONG WOMAN

I haven't always viewed myself as strong. What I know now is that I was wrong.

I am strong with my vulnerability. Knowing that this is a super strength in the world and knowing myself well enough that I can show up as me.

I am strong in how I recognize when my body or soul is asking for a rest and taking the time to practice self-care. I know now that this is not showing defeat or weakness. I know it is necessary in helping to avoid illness and burnout and that I am worthy of stepping out of the busyness sometimes.

I am strong enough to take time to cry when I feel like I need to. Being strong isn't about having things together all of the time. It's about facing emotions or challenges with grace and ease.

I am becoming stronger by asking for and accepting support. This is a new one for me. I am stronger for pushing out of my comfort zone.

I am strong and perfectly imperfect

UNDEFINED

The things that happen in our lives
are not defining moments
they do not speak of our character
they do not voice our soul

we all have moments we wish we could forget
re-live
but remember the profound way

you have grown because of, not in spite of

LESSONS

A chill in the air that reminds you that the sun doesn't shine everyday. Sometimes the wind blows and makes life messy. And the leaves, the leaves show us that it's ok to let go. As they let go and drop from the supportive branches that they cling to. Sometimes it's ok to let go. All the colors change around us. It's ok to change, transform, and not look back. The lessons are all around us.

JOURNEYS INWARD

Now's the time
heal that heart
remove those chains
take off the armour

Heal

don't be afraid of the emotions
rain is cleansing as it pours down your face
put down the heavy rocks
you collected as a child

Feel

forgive yourself
and the demons that held you down
covered up your screams
release it into the wind
disintegration
break it down-let it go

Release

you aren't your trauma

it doesn't own you
it's ok to be broken for a little while
it won't be that way forever

Surrender

Chapter Three
Changing Seasons

I AM HER

I catch a glimpse of your smile from across the room
only yours is kept behind glass
forever etched in time
timeless beauty

I recognize your face as if I am looking at my own reflection
same expressive eyes, same button nose
I wonder what your time was like

what made your heart sing?
did you dance in the moonlight?
sway to the rustle of the leaves?

I feel your essence blended with mine
your warm embrace that cradles my soul
everything I have been searching for
I have found kept behind this crystal

I feel a warmness running down my face
"I am her" I hear my inner voice say
"She is me" I hear being whispered in return

Flakes Of Wonder

Flakes of wonder fall from the sky

each different from the next

they land on my eyelashes

and turn into a gentle tear

WINTER MAGIC

The world falls away
exposing the shadows
that were bathed in glory
now is the time to rest
to come home

newness is birthed
quietly in the dark
a time for soul creations
as we hibernate
the sunshine coming from within

this is a time to nurture
body, mind and spirit
a time to share your light
into the vast darkness

let your light burn brightly
coming home to yourself

THUNDER AND LIGHTNING

The thunder rolls across the sky
loud and forceful
demanding to be heard and paid attention to
pent up and explosive

it remains unpredictable
it follows no rules
only bowing down to lightning
who leads the way through the skies

its bold and bright burst of light
turning the night skies into day
just for a split second
and then it's gone

it dances across the dark canvas
the opening act
graceful and illuminating
quiet yet vivid

thunder and lightning
the perfect duo of power

LIFE

Coffee in hand
sun pouring in the windows
gentle piano tunes playing
it's mornings like this
that make life worth living

feeling my heart burning brightest
words pouring through my fingers
coming to life on the pages
it's mornings like this
that birth my passion to life

when everything feels possible
free to be, to exist
to take up space
to be seen
it's these moments when I most feel alive

COMING HOME

Autumn is a coming home
leaves falling to the earth
from which they were birthed
the fox returning to its den
its home
the flowers are called home
to rest and be still
I call my heart home
from the adventure of the summer
road trips and lake days
and sand that swallowed my toes
home, to harvest my experiences
and keep them warm within my soul

autumn is a coming home
answer that call
and return home

DEATH GRIP

I feel his cold hands from across the room
his wretched fingers running through my hair
he says that we are long lost friends
and he does seem quite familiar

his cold breath whispers in my ear
like a cold January wind
he caresses my cheeks
with his frigid tongue
leaving behind a wet trail
how familiar he seems

he binds my feet
not allowing me to flee
add weights to all of my limbs
too much effort required to struggle
his chains are cold against my flesh
keeping me safe from what's out there

I wish that I could fight him off with my inner fire
but I fear catching the flames myself
and burning this rickety structure to the ground

the only thing colder than ice is ash

Ocean Wishes

I send my wish into the great depths of the ocean, carried off by the surging tide

Snowflakes

Fingerprints of the sky

- Snowflakes

COLD RAIN

I love the rain
cold yet sweet
fresh yet dark

a beautiful juxtaposition

FLICKER OF THE WICK

I see you in the leaves
as they float melodically to the Earth
I feel you in the breeze
that moves in
swaying in the trees
as they prepare to rest

I hear you in the whisper of the night
your eyes in the twinkle of the stars
your face in the shadow of the moon
your encouragement in the flicker of the wick

A CHANGE OF SEASON

Maybe it's the cold, crisp air
the one that is palpable in the dark evenings
maybe it's the naked branches
exposed and left behind
maybe it's the inky black skies
gone are long summer nights
maybe it's the plumes of smoke
that rise from the chimneys
or the barren landscapes
once rich with greenery and blossoms

it's a season of shutting down
of turning in
and maybe that's what makes me
feel like I'm on the wrong side
of the fogged up window pane

COLD NIGHTS

The fires ferociously roar inside
warming my toes
filling my senses
staving off the cold of the night

Harsh Realization

To be as temporary as the letters written in the sand

- harsh realization

STILL HERE

They say you're gone, but how can you really be? There is an unfinished story in my thoughts and my dreams where you are still very much here. You live in each moment of joy and each moment of sorrow. Always there to offer your support. How can you really be gone?

I just talked to you today.

Distant

It's awfully cold

when you're far from the flames

GENTLE RAIN

As the rain falls
slow and gentle
it cleanses my soul
-a way to start anew

FLAMES OF THE SUN

The flames of the sun burn a little brighter
within the reflection of my iris

Life's Art Class

Rain
coffee
poetry
my Saturday art class

GRACE

Like the rain
I am looking for
a way to fall
without looking broken

-   Grace

RAIN CLOUDS

No one judges the rainclouds
the way they judge other people's tears

Writer's Mind

Sunshine

on my skin

poetry

on my mind

I am complete

WINTER NIGHT

The chill of winter
settles into my bones

THE COLORS OF FALL

Falling of the leaves
the night sky darkens early
smells of fireplaces in the air
reds and oranges paint the Earth's canvas
mornings are greeted with frost
fall

NEVER AFRAID

The leaves float down
never afraid to let go
as they know they will be back

HOME

Home is not a physical place
it's not the circumstances of location
it's the warm breeze gently blowing through my hair
it's in the smell of where my head finds your chest
in the sand that cradles my curious body

home is the soothing voice of a dear friend
it's hearing your favorite song gliding through the air
the sound of childish laughter filling the streets
it's the feel of steady rhythm in my chest
it's in the tips of your fingers as they graze my cheek
the way my morning coffee fills my senses

home can't be lost
can't be stolen away in the night
for it is in all the small wonders that grace our lives
those moments of feeling seen/heard/held

home is within all of us

SUNSHINE IN MY HEART

I'm not ready to let go of the summer nights
bright skies and warm air
sunshine washing over everything
I will hold you in my heart
until next year

KISS OF THE SUN

Offering your skin to the blazing sun
is a vulnerability in its own
the kiss of heat that sears the supple canvas
brightly exposing every dimple and scar
a power that soaks through
straight to the soul

UNAFRAID

I want to be unafraid
the way the leaves are
they change their colors
the way I wish I could

LITTLE WONDERS

Little wonders
in the dew drops of the early dawn
there's a breeze that floats by
with the whispers from the wind
sparking memories of days gone by

little wonders
in the brightness of the stars
peeking out from behind the cotton candy sky
impatient to light up the dark canvas
that drapes the windows of the day

little wonders
in the softness of fibres
caressing the chill from your skin
infiltrating into the lonely space
surrounding you
bringing forth a sense of home
warmth

little wonders

in the sounds of their voices
putting words and songs to the language of your soul
eloquently expressing joy; pain
providing a safe place to land

the little wonders are always there
even when there are shrouded by darkness
lift your heart to the sky
and listen
wait
watch

Chapter Four
Phases of the Moon

CELEBRATION OF WOMEN

Have you ever wondered 'who are the women who came
before me'? Of course you know some of them, but I mean
really really came before you. Centuries of wise and fierce
warrior women prelude us, and this is for them.

As I get ready to tuck in my tired feet for the night
before I draw the blinds
I peer out the window one last time

the majestic lady in the sky never lets me down
night after night she shines
even after the most devastating of days

I lap up the pale glow she sheds upon me
I think about the things and events she has seen in her lifetime
she knows the innermost secrets of all of us
she has seen what hides in the darkest of forests
this is the same moon that they spoke to in the night
they were bathed in this same cool glow

I think of the wild women, running free in the night
captured by the light of the flames

the ones who were healers
able to heal the hurt of many
with their warm hands and empowering words

the warrior women, holding strong
never cracking to the pressures that they endured
I wonder which one had these same green eyes
who had this heart filled with grace and fire

where do I get my tenacious spirit
and love for the magical things
who puts the messages in my realm
always taking care of me, from far beyond

I am all of them
every celebration marked by fire
every powerful intention
each healing recipe
and tradition
form each cell within me

I am the fear and the wild
the stubborn and the magic
they have invoked their ancient wisdom

and shared their many gifts and power
I celebrate and honor them

To The Moon

I tell you my secrets
dreams, desires
and you never tell another soul

-   To the moon

CARRY ME

Carry my tired bones
while I find the medicine to heal my soul

SECRETS

You encapsulate the secrets of the stars in your eyes
with each fleck of gold and green and blue
holding their wonder within you

the moon is deep within your skin
glowing outwardly into the world
shedding wisdom amongst this plain

the magic of the ocean is held within your fingers
the gentle caress of the tide
depth that has no end

it's all around you
me
us
we all embody the magnificent
the pure magic
the secrets

SHIVERS

My lips graze down your spine
waiting for the bumps to raise on your skin
because your body says what your words can't say

SPIRIT VISITS

I feel your spirit with me
on those quiet and lonely nights
when I just can't seem to shake it off
there you are with me

you never let me fall over the edge
you hold me up when I feel too heavy
you show me the love you always have
and remind me of where I come from

it's a magical thing
the way you always find my soul
when it most needs yours
forever bound

I reach out for your hand
which is never there
your presence is felt
but only with my soul

when I close my eyes, I see your face
smiling back at mine
reminding me of the wisdom
you have provided me with

our spirits sing a song that I can't hear
but I feel the vibrations in my heart

my body feels the healing power
and then you're gone

until next time

THE MESSENGER

Whispers
I hear their whispers in the night
being swept gently through the dark sky
why me?
why am I the one to hear all their stories?

ancient wisdom from lessons learned
tragic and lonely
searching for their solace and peace
reaching out for anyone who will listen

they have messages for their people
and I am the envelope that they tuck their letters in
scratched with the ink
twisted with the cursive of each word

-    The Messenger

WOLF MOON

She howls down at Earth
from her throne within the orbit
sky the darkest shade of navy
her power emanates

don't hold your gaze too long
unable to look away

she howls down
and something within
howls back

Bathing In The Moonlight

I gain my stories by bathing in the same moonlight
that has grazed your skin

STRAWBERRY MOON

I reach my eyes to the inky night sky
searching for some familiarity
to recognize my soul in the darkness
to be understood

I bathe in the full moon light
soaking in the medicine and wisdom
filling up on the wholeness she invokes
charging my inner compass
for the next part of the journey

I relish in the stillness of the air
listening for my next inspiration
the words floating around in the sky
surrounding the strawberry moon

the glow caresses my cheek
encouraging me on my journey
I am mesmerised by her gentleness
completely nourished from her charge

she sees me for who I am
no amount of disguise can make her see anyone else
she hears my voice and my whispers in the night
she sees the power in my heart

I feel
free/forgiven
understood/heard
held/cherished
ignited/driven

KEEPER OF SECRETS

Yellow sliver of luminosity
within the enchanting night sky
you are the keeper of all secrets
that are whispered in the night

JOYOUS REUNION

There are those who were called back too early
those who lived a long rich life
there are those who were lonely until the end
and the ones who would have traded anything for one
more day
one more hour

some of us are lost without you
others rejoice from the many years and memories created
some don't even know that they lost you yet
estranged
and those of us who would trade anything for one more
day
one more hour

we talk to you over our early morning coffee
we watch you dance in the sky with the lady of the night
we spend time with you in our dreams
we think about how you would look today
smell, sound, laugh
we miss you in our best days
and even more in our worst

we leave a seat for you at the table

a spot for you in our hearts
and as we get one day closer to seeing you again
we think about the joyous reunion
of the day when we will no longer be apart

until then, we miss you

THREADBARE MOON

Pale lonely crescent
dim in the night
too threadbare to cast your healing glow tonight
I admire your strength
to show up even when you don't feel whole

LA LUNA

Her beauty is one of a kind
always shedding her light
down onto the darkness
her glow always comes from within

her wholeness appears to be in phases
but even her crescent transition is enough
just another chapter on the path to fullness

whole

she never dulls herself
never shines "too bright"
sure of who she is
ruler of the skies

she guides those who are lost
those out at sea
she hears the secret whispers
shared with her in the night

La Luna is part of my soul
reminding me of my inner light
raw, real and whole
guiding us out of the darkness

FULL MOON

The moon in its fullness
brings out the werewolf in all of us
shapeshifters of the night
guided by the divine glow

the night bright enough
for us to carefully let our wolf parts show
the one night to be free
as all eyes direct to the sky
we lurk in the shadows

unseen

DRIFTING

Drifting
    floating
        wafting
            through the night sky air
            graceful like the moon
            untethered from my earthbound body

            don't send me back too soon

IMPACT

You just never know the impact
your gifts bring into the world
they bring peace to other souls
and inspiration to follow their dreams

it may be the words someone needed
in order to keep on breathing

shine your bright light into the world

UNTAMED MOON

she smiles down in the night
bringing light to all the dark places
her reach dives deep within the forest
bathing the wolves and the wild

DREAMS

I long to be the moon;
she has the honor of hearing all your dreams
breathed into the night

EYES OF THE MOON

The sun sees every freckle, every curve
it illuminates the vessel, the body

but the moon
she sees only that which cannot be seen
she sees the way you lie in bed
sleepless in the night
she sees your aspirations and dreams
and the emotions you try your best to shelter from the day

she has seen the longing
the loneliness
the unrequited love
the long lost lovers

for the sun takes in our body
and the moon greets our soul

About the Author

Kim Germsheid has been writing from a very young age and this is her debut poetry book. She grew up in small town Saskatchewan and relocated and settled into the Edmonton area.

She has always held an extensive collection of books of many genres. You can find Kim travelling, catching up with friends in coffee shops or roaming and discovering bookstores.

In early 2022, Kim lost nearly everything in a house fire. Most of her writing was in the form of pen and paper so a lot of her life's work was lost within the flames. This book is the collection of writing she has created since the fire with a consistent thread of fire, growth and rebuilding within her pieces.

You can find her work on Instagram and Facebook at @mrs.eddie.vedder and Kim Germsheid respectively. You can contact her at acollectionofashes@gmail.com.

KIM GERMSHEID

Manufactured by Amazon.ca
Bolton, ON

38221984R00085